YOUR MONEY. YOUR SLAVE. – BOOK 2:
Power to Save: Putting you on a path to financial prosperity

Table of Contents

Chapter 1

"The habit of saving is itself an education; it fosters every virtue, teaches self-denial, cultivates the sense of order, trains to forethought, and so broadens the mind." — T.T. Munger

Background

Money is a tool for us to use to meet some of our needs. It's the responsibility of an individual to plan and use it in a way to fulfill their goals and objectives. Many people struggle to carefully manage their income, and they often realize that they do not have any money left in their bank account at the end of the month. There are various reasons that people have given for not being able to save money. Many people do not earn enough money to meet all of their financial obligations. If you fall into that category, you should get Book 1 of this book series, *Power to Earn*, in order to learn how you can improve your earning potential. The other group of people that earn an above-average income and still find it challenging to keep some money for themselves are in that position because of the lack of power to save.

Power to Save is a book that will empower you to command your money by telling it where to go, when to go, what to do, and how hard it should work for you. The concept of commanding your money is simple but not easy. We live in a world of instant gratification; whenever we want anything, we want it right now. We want the latest iPhone whenever Apple rolls out a new model, and we are ready to buy the latest brand of a vehicle even when our two-year-old car is still running smoothly. We are constantly bombarded with promotions and advertisements for things we don't need. They lure us with discounts and limited-time offers, just so they can get their hands in our pocket. And we allow them to, just because we think we deserve to have these new shinning items. But the truth is that we lack control over our money.

When I was a young boy, my brother and I had the opportunity of going to the farm with my Dad on weekends. My father enjoyed farming and all those agricultural-related activities a lot. We had a shed where we kept all our belongings, and would take breaks whenever we got tired of the rigorous farming activities. My father hired laborers to help him till, cultivate, clear, and plant different seeds on the over twenty acres of land that my grandfather gave to him. The highlight of my farming adventure then was really the lunchtime, where we would go back to the shed and eat different exotic bush meats that were typically supplied by the local hunter in my village. I also enjoyed diving and swimming in the pool as a way of cooling off just before the close of the day.

At that young age, farming to me was mainly about fun and food, but many years down the line, I discovered that farming can also teach the concept of saving. In the beginning of the farming season, a farmer will take a portion of whatever seeds he plans to grow and plant it in the soil. In the harvest time, the farmer will gather the crops for consumption and selling, and he will keep a certain portion that will act as seeds for the next planting season. The farmer will not eat or sell all of his produce; otherwise, he will be left with nothing for the next planting season. The lesson from the farmer and the farming cycle can be applied directly to the principle of earning and saving money.

In the first book in this series, I established the fact that everyone needs to work in order to earn a living. I shared the different types of quadrants that are available for you to make money, and I gave some recommendations that can help you earn extra income if you are finding it hard to make ends meet. Now that you are working and making some money, it is time to learn how to save a portion of your income. Just as the farmer wouldn't eat all of his produce from a harvest, you shouldn't spend all of your monthly income on your personal upkeep or on certain other commitments. The portion you put in savings is meant to be invested so that your money can also work for you.

The more you can keep in savings and invest in a safe and reliable investment vehicle, the more money you'll be able to put to work for you, and the quicker you will be able to become financially free. This book aims to equip you and teach you the mindset needed to save money and build a solid financial foundation for a secured future.

What if you can start exercising your power over your money? What if you become more intentional about how you spend your money? What if you can get to a position where you can easily save

10% or even over 40% of your income? What's happened is you have acquired the power to save. You have gained control over your money, and you are on your way to making money your slave. Use this book as your tour guide to navigate through your journey, as you escape those traps that want to take your hard-earned money away from you. Here's to gaining back control of your money!

Who this book is for

"I work hard, but find it harder to save any money at the end of the month."

This is a common statement that I often hear from hardworking professionals whenever we talk about money. According to *GoBanking Rates' survey, close to 70% of Americans have less than $1,000 in savings, and almost half of the respondents to the survey said they have $0 in a saving account. Many claimed that if they could just get a higher salary, then they would be able to save more money. The truth is that if you cannot save $10 from an income of $1,000, then it will still be difficult to save $100 from an income of $10,000.

Many Americans find it challenging to save money, irrespective of their income level. So, if you're tired of living paycheck to paycheck, and if you're ready to take control of your money and always ensure that you have some money in your bank account at the end of the month, consider this book your blueprint to saving more money. This eBook will teach you how to create a spending plan, track your income, and how to command your money by telling it where to go, when to go, and what to do for you. Welcome to your Power to Save.

*https://www.gobankingrates.com/saving-money/savings-advice/americans-have-less-than-1000-in-savings/

Chapter 2

The art of saving

According to T.T Munger, "The habit of saving is itself an education; it fosters every virtue, teaches self-denial, cultivates the sense of order, trains to forethought, and so broadens the mind."

Our educational institutions have already failed when it comes to teaching people how to save money, so it has become an individual's responsibility to learn how to save and use their savings to build real wealth. This eBook is that education — your *Savings 101* — that will empower you with the sense of order that is essential for saving money.

Saving is an act that everyone needs to practice regularly until it becomes a habit. The good news is that you can start from where you are today, and practice to increase your saving rate until you reach the optimum level that fits your plans and goals.

First, let's look at two myths people associate with saving:

Myth 1: I cannot save money until I attain a certain level of income.

Fact 1: This is not totally true. If you can understand that saving is important, and you make it a priority, you will do anything you can to make sure you set some money aside as savings from your income. Where there is willpower, there will always be a way.

Myth 2: After taking care of all my living expenses there is nothing left to save.

Fact 2: This is like putting the cart before the horse. You must first save before you spend, and not the order way around.

I won't dispute the fact that savings rates can vary depending on living expenses and income. While some people may be able to save 30% of their income, others may be more comfortable with saving just 5%, while some other people will still struggle to save 1%. Anyone can begin from where they are and start saving a percentage or certain amount from their income until it becomes a habit. I have worked with someone in the past that was only able to save $1. With continuous help and mentoring, this individual is now able to save 5% of her income.

In my eBook *Money Equation*, I explained that there are two sides to your money: the income side and the expenses side. The book covered different ways to reduce your expenses so that you can always have surplus at the end of each month. Below is the money equation for you to understand the concept.

MONEY EQUATION

- **INCOME – EXPENSES = SAVINGS**
- **FINANCIAL PROPERITY = INCOME > EXPENSES**
- **DEBT = EXPENSES > INCOME**
- **PAYCHECK TO PAYCHECK (RAT RACE) = INCOME = EXPENSES**

In this book, however, I want you to put yourself first, and to do that, you must make saving a priority.

2.1 The concept of paying yourself first

"Pay yourself first. You work hard for your money, so it is reasonable to ensure that your money work hard for you in return." Those were the words of my one-time financial coach, during the first ever financial seminar that I attended many years ago. I attended the training when I began my career, as I was curious to know more about how to properly manage money. Before then, no one had ever taught me the concept of gaining financial freedom through savings. I knew I had to save a portion of my income, but I did not know the next step after that, nor did I understand that paying myself first was a way of saving money.

So why or how should you go about paying yourself first? The whole goal of paying yourself first is to ensure that you have some amount of money that you can use to build wealth and possibly create passive income in your portfolio. This amount should be added to the expense column in your budget and should be set up the same way as your monthly expenses — such as rent, food, and transportation — are set up. The only difference is that the savings will be going into a dedicated savings account that you will only use to invest.

When you receive a paycheck, the first thing to do is to set aside a certain percentage of the pay and transfer it into your savings account that you set up for this purpose. To make it easier for you, you can set up a direct deposit into this account with the rest of your salary going into your regular account. If possible, you can give this account a name — "Not to spend account," for example — and you should make it difficult for you to access this bank account, like an online bank without any physical location or ATM machine around you.

If you are falling short every month, don't go into debt or use a credit card. Consider cutting your expenses, or find other ways to boost your income. The goal here is to make this practice become a habit, and even if you cannot save a significant portion of your salary, you can start with ten dollars or even a dollar.

This concept may be simple, but it's hard to follow. It will be simple for those who already have the mindset and who understand the importance of paying themselves first, but it will be hard for those who are still struggling financially, people that are working low-paying jobs, and people with high amounts of debt. How do I expect them to save money when what they earn is not even enough to take care of their immediate needs? How can a man earning minimum wage ever save money for a secured future?

At this point, some people will say this is not possible to do, and they will close the book and continue in their old ways. You cannot win with a victim mentality, and you should not join the masses that believe that the system is rigged against them, those that have accepted that they cannot get ahead in life. You need a winning mindset in order to excel in anything you do, especially with your finances.

People have a misconception about saving money, especially towards retirement. Many wrongly believe that they need to be able to save a million dollars to become financially free. That million-dollar bar is keeping many people from even starting to put money aside towards savings, and the fear is that it is not possible for $100 to ever grow into a million dollars. The good news is you do not have to save a million dollars to retire, because people are in different situations and stages in life, with different income levels, from different family sizes, and they live in different locations with completely different lifestyles. For example, you can rent a two-bedroom apartment in Little Rock, AK for just $900 per month. A comparable unit in San Francisco, CA would set you back more than $4,000. That is why I will not recommend any specific amount of money as your saving goal. Rather, we will go with percentage of your income.

Ideally, it is good to save between 10% to 20% of your income. If you do this for many years and you find a suitable form of investment to make your money grow, your chance of becoming financially free will significantly improve. Still understanding that we are all in different financial situations, I will recommend you start from the maximum amount that you can put aside — which will cause you some discomfort. This may mean you will skip your morning coffee, drive a jalopy car, or live in a cheaper apartment. Basically, you may need to downgrade your life and live as cheaply as possible. With the situation of our economy today, with huge student loan debt, high auto loans, and enormous credit card debt, it is difficult for everyone to start with the 10% saving rate and still be able to service their other debts, too.

Paying yourself first really works, and anyone can do it. You just need to be intentional and become a little bit more organized in order to set this up and allow it to run on autopilot. As stated earlier, if you are in debt, you need to ensure that paying off your debt is in your focus, and you still need to find ways to pay yourself, even if it is just $1 from every paycheck. When you have paid off all your debts, you can scale up the amount you save closer to the recommended 10% to 20%, as you will have developed the discipline and learned the habits of saving money. At this stage, you will also be able to improve your lifestyle, drive a better car, and live in a better neighborhood because you have no debt left.

One of my favorite quotes is by Will Durant, which says, *"We are what we repeatedly do. Excellence, then, is not an act, but a habit."* When I think about my life and my financial journey, I can easily and emphatically conclude that developing the habit of paying myself first was instrumental to setting me up for a life of financial freedom. This quote placed an emphasis on the value of repetition and conforming to certain routine.

I want you to develop the habit of repeatedly paying yourself first and make it such a routine that it comes naturally to you. This is the principle that I adopted, and appreciate even now as I make progress in my financial planning. The good news is that anyone and everyone can develop the discipline and habits that will make them prosper financially.

Next, I will introduce a tool that will help you achieve the prosperity you desire.

2.2 Command your money: How to create a budget that works

A budget is an estimate of your income and expenditure that covers a particular period of time, typically a month. Most people receive their income on a monthly basis and as a result, they allocate the amount they plan to spend out of their income on a month-to-month basis. If you receive wages on a daily, weekly, or bi-weekly basis, though, the same concept still applies. Budgeting allows you to properly allocate your income so that you can fulfill the various categories of your monthly expenses.

You must make sure that you are not just saving money for the sake of it; you must save with a purpose in your mind. What do you plan to achieve with the money you are saving? If you have a purpose for the money you are saving, you will be able to stay focused and achieve your goal.

Your money goal can be short term, typically less than six months, which may involve saving to buy a TV or replace a broken appliance. It may be a medium-term savings goal, which may cover items like buying a new car or setting money aside for the down payment on your home — this can take anywhere between two to three years. You should also have a long-term savings goal to take care of your retirement or pay for your kids' college tuition. You must also have a goal for saving for emergencies, because unexpected events do occur. This should cover up to six months of your living expenses.

Commanding your money is a simple concept of controlling your money by telling it where to go at the end of each month, at the exact day you want it to go, as well as dictating what you want your money to do for you and how hard you want it to work for you in order to meet your needs. It is about making your money your slave. The simple tool for commanding your money is a budget and with it you can accomplish the following with your money.

Tell your money where to go and what to do

The budget lets you allocate your income into several categories to fit your needs. By using this tool, you are empowering yourself and telling your money exactly where you want it to go, and how much of it should go to each category.

The table below is a breakdown of how John Smith allocates his $3,500 monthly income for the month of July 2020.

Priority	Category	Amount
1	Savings	$200
2	Charity	$150
3	Food	$550
4	Housing	$1,050
5	Transportation	$380
6	Utility Bills	$470
7	Insurance and Taxes	$300
8	Debt Repayment	$250
9	Fun	$100
10	Other	$50

From the table above, it is clear that John made saving a priority. Although he is not able to save 10% of his income in the month of June, he is still able to save over 5% of his income while also fulfilling his other financial obligations. By setting up his budget this way, he is telling his money exactly where to go, and how much of it should go to each category. He is also able to command his money to tell it what to do once it gets to where it is allocated. With this budget, he was able to properly plan and allocate his money to fulfill his needs — like food and housing — in the order of his priorities.

Tell your money when to go

You can use the budget to not only tell your money where to go, but when exactly to go. If you are the type that overdraws your account from time to time, I will show you a trick that will help you put an end to that and save you the ridiculous $35 overdraft fee, based on the dates that you get your income, whether it is on a weekly, bi-weekly, or monthly basis. This exercise will take you about ten minutes to set up, and once you have it created, you can use it as a blueprint to distributing your income for subsequent months.

Priority	Category	Amount	Date
1	Savings	$200	June 1
2	Charity	$150	June 7
3	Food	$550	June 1
4	Housing	$1,050	June 3
5	Transportation	$380	June 5
6	Utility Bills	$470	June 20
7	Insurance and Taxes	$300	June 25
8	Debt Repayment	$250	June 28
9	Fun	$100	June 30
10	Other	$50	June 30

Using this template, you now have the ability to tell your service providers the date you want them to take out money from your account. If the dates are not aligned with your service plans, then you need to get them aligned, and here's a trick that will help you achieve this. Let's pick up the phone and call your service provider. You can borrow from my script to get you prepared.

Trick to know

My script to your providers

Customer Service Agent: Thank you for calling us. Am I on with John Smith?

You: Hello, Mr. Customer Service. This is John Smith. I would like to discuss my billing schedule with you.

Customer Service Agent: Hello, Mr. Smith. Thank you for using our service. How may I help you today?

You: I know I have other options out there, but I have been with your company for a while, so I want to stick around. I started following a new budget template, and I want to make sure that there is money in my account when you are ready to deduct my payment. Currently my billing cycle is every 14th of the month, but I would like to move it to the 20th of every month.

Customer Service Agent: That shouldn't be a problem. I can easily manage that for you. However, I should let you know that your payment will be a little higher this month because we are extending the payment date by about a week. But everything will go back to your regular payment starting next month. Is that okay?

You: Thank you for your help. That will be just fine.

Customer Service Agent: Thank you once again for choosing us. Have a great rest of your day.

If the agent proves difficult, you should ask to speak with their manager, and let them know you have other choices if they don't honor your request.

Tell your money how hard to work

This is perhaps the most important thing you need to understand about money. You must find a way of making the money you save every month work hard for you. The harder it works, the richer it makes you. This is one of the core differences between the very rich and the poor. Rich people are not looking for higher salaries; rather, they are looking for investments that will continuously generate money for them, whether they work or not. Telling your money how hard to work for you is about investing your savings carefully in such a way that the savings will also provide more income for you. If you practice this for long enough, it is very possible to get to a point where your investments will produce the same income as you get from your active employment.

How to create a budget that works!

Creating a budget is not a difficult process. All it requires is some level of diligence and proper organization.

First, if you don't already know all your monthly expenses, you will need the following to get started:
- Bank account statement (3 months)
- Credit card statement (3 months)

The reason why you need those statements is to help you get organized and review your past expenses, which will ensure you create a budget that is accurate. After you have identified your past expenses, then you will put them into categories. Our ultimate goal is to create a zero-based budget, and add savings as a line item.

To make it easy, I have come up with four main categories:
1. Saving: This is the amount you want to set aside every month. This is the money you will use to build your income portfolio.
2. Essentials: This covers your expenses that are absolutely necessary for each month, like rent, food, transportation, and utilities.
3. End Game: This category includes monthly allocations towards the future. It includes saving for your retirement or college savings for your children (if you have any). This category provides you safety and security.
4. Extras: This category provides you comfort. Example includes personal spending for eating out, vacation, and charity donations.

ACTIVITY 1
TASK: Create your budget

2.3 The five commandments of saving money

There are principles to most good things in life. For example, if you want to keep a healthy weight, you have to exercise regularly and follow a nutrition regimen. If you want to grow your business, you should understand your customers, and serve them diligently by providing top-notch products and services. In the same way, if you ever want to understand the art of saving, you must know the core principles that will help you save more money.

In this section, I am calling those principles "the five commandments of saving money." If you learn and follow these commandments, you will gain the motivation and understanding of why saving money should be a priority — which will make it easier to start saving.

1. <u>Have a financial plan:</u> Most people around you probably have no financial plans. They just go with the flow. They try to buy a house when they see their colleagues buying one, and they want to buy a new car when they discover that the car manufacturer has rolled out a new model. They spend money without necessarily checking if and when they can afford the item that they want.

   If you want to learn how to save, you need to come up with a financial plan. The plan for your retirement — when you want to retire and the amount you want to have by the time you reach the retirement age. A plan for how big of a mortgage to have, and when to pay it off. A specific plan for how to save for your kids' college education, and for other related items that you need to spend money on.

   The purpose of having a financial plan is to prioritize when you put your budget together. For example, if you are thinking of buying a home, you know that you need to have a down payment for it. One of your goals in your financial plan will be to save money for the down payment. If any other wants pop up out of nowhere, your motivation and desire to own your home will help you stick to your goal as laid out in your financial plan.

2. <u>Make saving a priority</u>: The rich save, then spend. The average man tries to save after spending. Making saving a priority means that you must follow the right order: don't try to save what's left over after spending, but spend what's

left over after saving some money. As we learned above, if you are not already used to saving, or if you are still struggling financially to make ends meet, you may find this difficult initially. But when you start gradually, your brain will readjust, and you feel excitement, not pain, whenever you set aside certain amounts for saving.

3. Turn your savings into income producing tool: Saving money is not your ultimate goal. Making your money work very hard so that it will become an income-generating tool is where you want to be — a position where you make money even while sleeping. All the money that you save should therefore be channeled towards investments that will consistently and persistently produce returns for you.

    Let's assume that you have decided to build wealth through real estate property investments. If you want to buy a rental apartment at a cost of $80,000, you need to have at least 20% of the total cost as your down payment. That means you must come up with $16,000 to pay for the property. How long will it take you to save $16,000?

    By saving $1,000 every month, you will have $16,000 in 16 months.
    By saving $500 every month, you will have $16,000 in 32 months.
    By saving $250 every month, you will have $16,000 in 64 months.

    Most people won't be able to do this because of the time frame. In a world of instant gratification, we want what we want right now! The truth is that the first investment property is always the most challenging one. If it took you 32 months to save the down payment for your first property, the second one may take just about 24 months, because the income from the first property is now being added to your savings. Instead of saving $500 per month, you are now able to save about $700 every month. The third property will take even lesser time, because you are generating income from two properties.

I know a friend that used this method to acquire 10 properties within 15 years. He was not a high-income earner by any means. He was just passionate, very disciplined, and focused on the goal of owning rental properties. You too, my friend, can do it. It doesn't necessarily have to be rental properties. You can decide to invest in the stock market or any business for that matter, but make sure your money is working very hard to make more money for you.

4. <u>Be a conscious spender</u>: Spending money out of control is a recipe for living paycheck to paycheck and being poor. To be a conscious spender means to know where your money goes, when it goes, and to have a purpose for what you need your money to do. You cannot thrive by being a spontaneous spender. If you earn $400 per day as an income, and if you find yourself buying shoes that cost $800, you need to ask the question, "Is this shoe really worth two days of hard work?" A conscious spender carefully plans their spending using a budget, and establishes a purpose for what they are spending on, to make sure it aligns with their overall financial plans. Conscious spending is not about being cheap. It's about knowing what you want, why you want it, and making sure that you're getting a good value on what you spend your money on.

5. <u>Think future</u>: If you can ask your future self a question before you make your next purchase, you will get a perspective of whether or not what you are purchasing makes sense. Your future self may be able to guide you and make you realize that there are other more important things you could do to prepare for a future you will enjoy, and which you will be proud of. What kind of tomorrow do you want? Do you want a future where you have money coming to you whether or not you work? Do you want to create a future where you are self-sustaining, and not depending on the government — or anyone, for that matter — for your financial needs?

You can start creating that future today by always checking with your future self if he or she will be proud of what you are spending your money on today. Don't go through life as if there is no tomorrow and planning as if you will live forever. Planning your budget, thinking strategically about your finances, and following money principle is a good way to put the future in focus as you make saving money a priority.

ACTIVITY 2
TASK: Create your financial plan

2.4 Points to note about saving money

Below are some points to note when you start saving money:
- To win with your money you have to make saving a priority.
- Saving money may be difficult initially, but when you practice it for a long time it can become a habit.
- You must save with a purpose. You are not just setting aside money to make sure you have money in your bank account. You must have plans and a purpose for the money you are saving.
- Don't save what is left after spending. Rather, spend what is left after savings.
- You must find ways of using your savings such that it will produce passive income streams for you.
- Use your savings to build your investment portfolio and create passive income.
- Plan your money so that your future self will be grateful for your current self.

Success requires discipline. Budgeting and saving money is a process of becoming a disciplined manager of your money. Stay committed and you will win.

Chapter 3

Intentional Spending

Check out the statements below:
- I have no idea where all my money goes at the end of every month.
- I earn so much, but I find it so hard to save. I can never stop working.
- Oops, I did not check the price tag. I think I overpaid for those shoes.

The statements above are some of the comments that you'll hear from people who are not intentional about their spending. These people surely know how to make money, but they lack the willpower or the intentionality to control their money. They do not have the power to save. Their inability to step up and take control of their money often leaves them broke and always needing to make more. If they get a pay raise, they still find themselves struggling to properly account for their money, not knowing where the money went at the end of the month, or why they always have to pay bank fees for overdrawing their accounts.

Being able to spend at will is one of the many reasons why people work to earn an income. Our fundamental obligations to take care of our personal needs means we must spend money in order to fulfil those obligations. We need food to sustain our lives, therefore we must spend money on groceries. We need a pace to relax, unwind, and sleep at the end of the day, hence the need for spending on housing. We need to go from one place to another as we seek our daily bread and to care for our loved ones, necessitating the need to spend on transportation. We all want and desire the good things of life, which make us spend money to acquire them. The big question is how can you be a conscious spender? How do you ensure that you are spending at a level appropriate for your income?

Tammy B and Tiffany K are good friends.

Tammy B, an investment banker, earns $550,000 every year. She lives in a beautiful five-bedroom house in one of the most affluent neighborhoods in the city. She just bought the latest BMW X7 at a cost of $82,000.

Tiffany K, a medical doctor who earns $280,000 every year, also lives in a pretty decent neighborhood. She got a little uneasy when she learned that Tammy had just bought a BMW X7. She said to herself, if she can get it, I can too.

Can Tiffany afford it?
I enjoy Suze Orman's show, especially the segment where she asks her guest if they can afford what they are intending to buy. She will then ask them to show her the money. She will look at their income, debt, and financial standing before deciding whether the caller can afford the item or not.

To me, "Can you afford it?" is about being intentional in your spending. It is a way of making sure that you live within your income, and making sure that you put saving as a priority. If you are a conscious spender, your lifestyle will be measured based on your income, and not that of your friend or next-door neighbor. That way, if you are on an income of $75,000 per annum, you will not become uneasy just because your friend who earns $250,000 just bought a new boat.

You'll learn not to measure your life, your accomplishments, or material possession based on someone else's yardstick. You'll know for sure what you can afford, when you can afford it, and — most importantly — if it aligns with your personal financial goal. Intentional spending is a way of empowering yourself to take control of your money and be a good steward of the resources that God has provided to you.

Can you afford it?
Ask yourself these questions:
1. Can I afford it?
2. Is this spending commensurate to my income level?
3. Is this spending aligned with my personal financial goal?

Rich but poor. Poor but rich.

Looks can be very deceiving, especially when you consider what's going on in our society today. We now live in an era where people thrive in debt. They live on borrowed money to impress the naïve people around them, who look up to them as the epitome of what a rich life should look like. If only they knew that the rich man was nothing but poor. If only they knew that he is in debt to his teeth, and that he cannot sleep peacefully without thinking about the amount that he owes. Of course, if they did, more people would realize that these fake lives are superficial and not the best way to live.

Our society measure success based on outward appearances: who drives the best cars, who lives in the richest zip codes, and who wears the most expensive line of clothing. We don't care to ask if they can actually afford it. We don't want to know if they are in debt just so that they can maintain their fake lifestyle. But things don't always end nicely for these people, and after a while, just like dominoes, the sham that they built will come falling down.

Sylvia Bloom was a legal secretary from Brooklyn who worked for the same law firm for 67 years while quietly accumulating a fortune unknown to many of her friends and family. Sylvia was thrifty, She took the subway to work each day, and lived with her husband in a rent-controlled apartment. But Sylvia had quietly amassed over $9 million through a string of investments she made while she was alive — a silent millionaire by all accounts. She left more than $6 million dollar to Henry Street, a social service provider supporting college education for disadvantaged students. She appeared poor, but was actually rich.

That is the case of most everyday millionaires around you. They may not drive the latest cars, or live in the most affluent part of the city, but they have used the power to save to build wealth that will last a long time.

The question to ask now is which path do you want to take? Do you want to be the fake millionaire with huge debts, or the silent millionaire with huge wealth? The latter is a better option, and to get there, you need to be intentional with your spending. You should use your power to save to control your spending.

Don't be cheap. Be frugal.

Most people confuse being cheap with frugal, but there is a clear difference. Being frugal means, you want more value for your money, but a cheap person always tries to pay the lowest price, regardless of value. For example, a cheap person will most likely be willing to drive to twenty different stores when they want to buy an item just because they can save five cents. They are driven by the need to spend less money.

A frugal person, on the other hand, wants to maximize total value by buying only things that they need at a relatively reasonable price without compromising other important things that they care about. The cheap person that drove to twenty stores to save five cents has probably unconsciously lost money by expending more fuel in their car, and has, of course, wasted more of their time.

You are cheap if you:
- Only care about the price of the item you are buying, irrespective of the quality.
- Always want to buy the lowest cost item.
- Don't care how long it takes you to find the lowest price.
- Find it hard to part with your money.
- Have a scarcity mentality, and avoid spending.

You are frugal if you:
- Understand that it is better to pay more sometimes in order to get better value.
- Put people above savings. You would rather use a coupon so that you can tip the server.
- Explore ways to save money without sacrificing your lifestyle.
- Be disciplined and a good steward of money.

Both the frugal and cheap people love to save money, but frugal people will not do so at the expense of others. They will not cheat or put others at a disadvantage just so they can save money. Frugal people will consider it a great deal to pay a little more for a quality mattress so that they can avoid discomfort and enjoy a good night sleep. But cheap people will only want to buy the cheapest mattress in the store regardless of the long-term effect on their lives.

It's okay to be frugal. In fact, you'll be in the company of one of the richest people in the world: Warren Buffett. He drives the same car for many years, and still lives in the same house that he bought in the 1960s. Warren could afford to buy the latest and best of all these material things if he chose to do so, but he believes in frugality, and loves to get value for his money.

The Financial Independence, Retire Early (FIRE) movement has also popularized frugality. The FIRE movement consists of Millennials who are bucking the traditional belief that you must work until you are 65. They have the goal to save and invest very aggressively, and most of the time, save over 50% of their income. As such, some of them are now retiring at age 45. The reason why they are able to achieve this goal is that they made saving a priority, live well below their income, and saved aggressively. Becoming frugal and controlling your expenses can help you quickly attain financial freedom.

Peaceful living. Content journey.

We are under intense pressure to always spend much more than we make. This is the rationale that gets us in trouble, where many years of uncontrolled, unconscious spending puts us in the cage of debt, and we have to continuously work in order to keep up with our high tastes and expensive lifestyle. Meanwhile, we are gradually approaching age 50, with only a meagre amount in our retirement portfolio. Fear will begin to set in: fear of layoff, fear of running out of money, and fear of not having enough at retirement. Very soon, the fear will turn into resentment and hatred. We are now jealous of our younger colleagues that seem to understand the importance of saving, and who appear to be on track to retire rich. We feel animosity towards our employers for not paying us high enough, and resentment towards the government for not doing enough to protect us.

But we don't need fear at this point. Fear will only stop us from looking in the mirror and taking responsibility for our actions. Instead we need to learn how to take control, which is what

Chapter 4 of this book will cover. We also need to live in peace and be content with what we have.

Peaceful living puts you back in control as you learn to command your money as laid out in Chapter 2. Peaceful living will help you put things in the right perspective and know that you are not in any race with your friends or colleagues in the office. If your friend just bought a new Ferrari F8 Tributo, you are at peace because your ten-year-old Toyota serves the same purpose to take you from one point to another. Peaceful living helps you to realize that even though Apple just rolled out the latest iPhone, you are not under any pressure to buy it as long as your iPhone 8 still serves its purpose to make and receive calls. You are living in peace when the teasing advertisement on your TV for a limited time offer for something you do not really need does not lead you to dip into your savings and rob your future self of your potential wealth.

Peaceful living is about you creating your benchmark for what you want and when you want it, and ensuring that you can afford it. It means you are at peace with yourself. It, however, does not mean you are devoid of ambitions and aspirations — you are just not judging yourself based on someone else's yardstick. It means you live your life according to your personal goals and plans, and consequently, you manage your finances to reflect the power to live according to your standard.

Peaceful living creates contentment because it helps you to show gratitude by recognizing the blessings in your life. It means you may not have everything you desire yet, but you appreciate and are grateful for those things you currently have. It also helps you to think of others that are less fortunate than yourself. I like the saying, "I complained that I had no shoes until I met a man who had no feet." This means, if you are complaining that you live in a one-bedroom apartment, know that the guy that lives in his car would love to have that room. Peaceful living helps you to think less of yourself and it fosters happiness and contentment. It helps you to count your blessings.

ACTIVITY 2
TASK: Create your contentment journal. What are you grateful for?

Chapter 4

4.1 Take Control. You are not a victim.

Personal finance is about control. Many people have bought into the victim mentality when it comes to managing their finances because they believe that they have limitations on what they can make and that they can't get ahead in life. This imaginary bar has to be broken in order for you to live to your full potential and be who God has created you to be. I want you to know that you are not a victim. You can boost your earnings potential so that your income can increase. And you can make money from any of the four quadrants that was described in Volume 1 of this series. If you are working as an employee today, and your income level is not commensurate with your experience, you know you deserve more. See the situation as only temporary. Don't stay there for too long and allow bitterness to set in. You can do something about it, like switch quadrants and start your own business. You do have options — you only have to look and explore all possibilities.

People go to their doctors for routine checks to ascertain the state of their health: the right level of blood cells, blood glucose level, blood pressure, and also to know if they are underweight, obese, or if they fall in the normal zone. The same principle applies when it comes to money management. Are you financially fit?

4.2 Financial fitness checkup

Many people are aware that they need regular exercise to keep physically fit. So they hit the gym, control their diet, walk, jog, or run, with the primary goal of staying healthy and enjoying a quality life. Just like you need regular exercise to keep fit, you also need a financial fitness checkup to gain or maintain control of your money and ensure that you are moving towards your overall financial goals.

Millions of people work hard to earn their money, but most don't perform any financial fitness check that will ensure that they become the master of their money. They don't have any earning, spending, or savings plans, making it difficult for them to achieve their financial goals.

Just as it's essential to be physically healthy, it is also crucial to ensure that you have sound financial wellness. How can we achieve this? By doing what we can to ensure that we are not spending more than we make, avoiding debt, and making our money work for us.

Here's a look at some ways to achieve financial wellness:

1. Become a money manager: You manage your physical wellness by ensuring that you get regular exercise and eating the right food. In the same way, you can achieve financial fitness by learning how to manage your money the right way. Learn to keep track of your income and expenses, and know the exact amount you spend on various categories of your expenses every month. Becoming active in managing your money will prevent you from wondering where your money went at the end of each month, and it will help you to properly plan and allocate your income based on your priorities.

Becoming a money manager does not mean you should literally become a professional money manager in an investment firm! It just means becoming conscious of what you spend, how you spend, and how to save and invest so that your money will ultimately work for you. Budgeting will help you take control of your money and ensure you are spending your money in a way that will make it easier to achieve your financial goals.

2. Avoid debt like the plague: Debt is an obligation to the past which will rob you of potential opportunities in the future. By going into debt, you're making other people richer with the interest you pay. According to the Federal Reserve, outstanding consumer debt exceeded the $4 trillion mark for the first time back in February 2019. This debt is preventing a lot of people from realizing their goals. To become financially fit, you need to avoid debt, or pay off all your debts if you already have them.

Debt steals from your future, and to have a financially sound future, you need to get rid of credit card debt, auto loans, payday loans, or any form of consumer debt to reduce and eliminate the interest being charged against you every month.

3. Right-size your income: When someone that is planning to lose weight goes to the gym, they should know the amount of weight they need to lose if they are going to see any results. An exercise routine will not be effective if this person just says, I am going to the gym, and I plan to lose weight. Consider another approach: I am going to the gym, and I plan to lose 10 pounds of weight within two months.

In the same way, for you to achieve financial wellness, you must be able to know the income level that is right for you. When most people are trying to accomplish any financial goal, the first thing they do is to cut back on their expenses. While this is okay to do, it's not always the best and most efficient approach. To right-size your income means to determine the appropriate income that will help to attain and sustain your desired standard of living, and also help fund a lifestyle that you want in retirement.

If you know that an income of $75,000 will be sufficient for you to live your life to your desired standard, you will struggle to balance your budget or fulfill your financial goals if your current income is only $50,000. To eliminate the struggle, you should find ways of generating more money so that you 'll be able to live the kind of life you love. If on the other hand, your income level is $100,000, you'll be able to quickly achieve your financial goals with careful planning, because that is $25,000 above your sufficiency level.

You can't achieve financial fitness by accident. You must have specific goals, and you must determine the income level that will help you fulfill those goals.

4. <u>Focus on your big goal</u>: When it comes to getting your finances in shape, you should endeavor to focus on the big goal. When you go to the gym for exercise, you tailor your exercise regimen to suit your fitness goals — whether it's losing weight or building your muscles.

Similarly, when it comes to your finances, you should have a goal, and then on a month-to-month basis, plan your money in such a way that you are moving towards your big goal. For example, if your big goal is to buy a car, or save a down payment for your house, you should allocate your money so that it will be more impactful in areas that are most important to you.

If you overspend on categories that are not important to you, you won't have any money left to fulfill your most important desires. So, put your focus and priority on your big goals, take small steps every month, and you will be able to attain financial fitness.

5. <u>Contentment is important</u>: In a world where everyone wants to keep up with the Joneses, it's too easy to get carried away and try to be like everyone else. In the gym, if you aim to build muscle, you know you have to lift weights to achieve your goal. But maybe you then meet someone else in the gym whose goal is to lose weight, and this person's workout schedule is to use the treadmill and perform some aerobic exercise. If you decide to copy this person and start walking on the treadmill instead of lifting weights, you'll fail to achieve your fitness goal.

Unfortunately, in terms of financial fitness, most people do not have goals, so they just blindly copy what others are doing. If your personal goal towards financial wellness is to get out of debt by paying off your credit card, you will struggle financially if you then decide to buy a new car just because a close friend just did.

You need contentment to achieve a life of financial wellness. Contentment is about setting your own goals, singing and dancing to your own tune, and not getting derailed by your next-door neighbor's melodious rock and roll. It is about identifying what is most important to you and staying in your own lane. It's refreshing to see more and more millennials getting caught up to the frugality movement such as FIRE (Financial Independence, Retire Early).

6. Influence what you can control – no excuses: On the few occasions when I go to the gym, I'll find some folks that are just there to create distractions. They came there for chitchat, and they won't follow the simple gym rules and etiquette. They are always noisy, they'll never put equipment away properly for the next user, they don't respect other people's space, and they typically display all sorts of obnoxious characters. I'm sure you have met people like these before, whether in the gym or in the pool, or elsewhere. They are unnecessary distractions, and most of the time, you cannot control them.

Regarding your finances, there are also so many things that are outside of your immediate control: the taxes you pay, the prevailing interest rates, companies' policies, and benefits program. The best way to live happily and achieve financial wholeness is to seek to influence only those things you can control. For example, you can control where you work. If you are not happy working with a particular company, you should have the courage to make the necessary change. If you have a government that is not implementing policies that are favorable to you, you should not just complain, you should vote and get people that represent your views in positions of authority.

7. Make your money your slave: When you go to the gym, you burn calories while expending your energy using the gym equipment: running on the treadmill, lifting a weight, or even by just doing your press up. The more energy you use, the more the calories you burn, and the healthier you get.

The reverse is the case when we consider financial fitness. Working longer hours or harder will not necessarily make you richer. The most hard-working people are not always the wealthiest people, but if you can learn how to work smarter and make your money work for you, then you'll be able to put yourself in a position to earn more money without putting out further effort. That is how the rich get richer.

This is the time to deploy the money that you have saved in Step Two into profitable investments that will continue to provide good returns to you year in and year out, rain or shine, so that you are making money whether you are sleeping or you are awake. To join the elite club of the rich, you should also find ways to generate passive income from multiple income streams. It is often said that an average wealthy person has more than five income streams. It is time to build your income streams and make your money your slave.

So, what's your status? Are you financially fit? Are you budgeting and controlling your money? Is the weight of debt holding you back and preventing you from reaching your goals? Let's take control and do something about it.

4.3 It's time to kill debt

Debt is a huge burden and a drag not only on the people in debt, but on society in general. For those in debt, they will not be able to plan or spend as they desire because of the unnecessary limitations that debt puts on them.

For example, take someone who earns a monthly salary of $3,500. If this person has no debt, he can plan on the entire income. If, however, he has multiple debt obligations which add up to about $1,000 — a student loan, an auto loan, credit card debt, or any other consumer debt — then his income is automatically limited because of the debt. He will only be able to plan on $2,500. He still has to take care of the essentials, such as housing, food, transportation, and utilities. If debt obligation is not promptly and aggressively addressed, it can linger for a very long time, which will perpetuate the debtor in a continuous debt spiral.

Imagine a person that took out an auto loan of 72 months on a five-year-old car. By the time this person is ready to pay off the car after the loan term, the car is also ready to be replaced. What does he do then? He goes to the dealership asking for another six-year loan on another car to replace the now old and rickety car. The end result is that he'll forever be in debt because he has not learned the concept of saving and planning money to accomplish his financial goals.

I had firsthand experience of the danger of debt when I first moved to America. As part of settling down, I went to Rooms to shop for furniture, and to my greatest surprise, they told me that I could pick any set of furniture that I wanted, with zero money down, and I could take five years to pay the furniture off. This is the greatest deal on earth, I said, in my naïve mind. It means I can have whatever I want, whenever I want it, without waiting to have the money! Who cares about delayed gratification when you can enjoy instant satisfaction.

So I picked the furniture I wanted. But in less than three years of use, it was ready for replacement. Meanwhile, I was still enjoying the low monthly payment that would last another two years. How can I get rid of something that I haven't finished paying for? That experience taught me the lesson that has saved me thousands of dollars that I would have paid in interest payments, because I said no more debt.

Since the US is a consumer-driven economy, the more people that are able to spend money, the healthier the economy gets, and vice versa. We have become accustomed to debt in this country, and we've accepted it as part of living in the richest country in the history of mankind. Check out America's debt profile:

- *Total student loan debt: $1.5T*
- *Total auto loan debt: $1.2T*
- *Credit card debt: Just surpassed $1T*
- *Total consumer debt: $4T (This is more than the GDP of India. India has a population of over 1 billion people, their GDP is $3.16T.)*
- *Total mortgage loan debt: ~$9T (More than the GDP of Japan, which is $5.36T.)*

- *US government debt: > $22T (Highest in the world)*

(Source: www.debt.org)

How can we boast about being the wealthiest nation on earth, yet are also the biggest debtor? How can we claim that we are a prosperous country, yet many of our citizens live paycheck to paycheck? You shouldn't look to the government for answers, as the US government has not done a good job managing its revenue.

The problem is yours to solve. Earning the appropriate income to maintain your lifestyle, managing your money properly using a budget, and getting out of debt will help set you on a path to financial prosperity.

There are two sides to the money equation: the income side and the expenses side. Many people focus only on cutting back their expenses in order to balance their budget, and that's okay, but you can only cut so much. The approach that I recommend is to make more money to enable you to maintain your lifestyle. That's what Volume 3 of this series is focused on. You need to be determined, you must be diligent, and really hate living in debt to kill debt. I did it, and so can you.

4.4 How to pay off your debt

To help guide you, here are my simple steps for beating debt and building wealth:

1. Save $2,000 for emergencies: Emergencies happen, and they occur when you least expect it. Appliances can breakdown without prior warning, car tires can blow up without asking for your permission. In order not to be caught off guard, you should save $2,000 as your emergency fund. Ideally, my preference is to have a total of one month's living expenses as your emergency fund. If anything unexpected happens, the fund in the emergency savings will take care of it without making you feel stressed or putting you in more debt.

2. Pay off your debts: Debt is your enemy, and it will prevent you from reaching your financial goals. It also makes you a

slave to the lender, because as you work hard, you are paying interest to the lender, making him richer. You should come up with a plan to pay off all your debts as soon as possible. Depending on the amount, you should set a goal to pay off everything (excluding your home mortgage) within two to three years.

To pay off your debt, follow the steps below. It is the snowball principle of paying debt.

> I.   *List all your debts.*
> II. *Arrange them in order from smallest to largest.*
> III. *Start paying the debts, starting with the smallest. If you have extra money, you should apply it towards the smallest debt. You must make minimum payments on all other debts.*
> IV. *After paying off the smallest, apply the money that you were paying on the smallest debt on the new smallest. Continue to make minimum payments on the other outstanding debts.*
> V.   *Repeat step IV until all debts have been paid off.*
> VI. *You did it! Have fun. Learn your lessons, and never go into debt again.*

3. <u>Make it a priority to save more</u>: At this point, you now have extra money that you can put towards savings. Make sure you save as much as possible. Ideally, you should target saving about 20% of your monthly income.
4. <u>Build a three-month reserve fund</u>: You should now build your emergency fund so it will cover your living expenses for three months or more. The purpose of this is so that you can take care of yourself, if you face any layoffs or career interruptions on your path.
5. <u>Invest and make your money your slave</u>: This is how the rich get richer. They invest their money, reinvest the returns, and continue for many years until their investments are sufficient to take care of their living expenses. Without any more debt, you are now in a position to invest like the rich. Make sure to study what you are investing so you won't lose your hard-earned money.

4.5 Automate to achieve peace of mind

The best way to ensure consistency in saving money is to automate it. You can automate your savings by ensuring that you save a portion of your income before it goes to into your regular account. This way you've already empowered yourself to pay yourself first before spending the rest of your income. You can give specific instructions to your employer to take out the portion you want to save and invest, thereby avoiding the temptation of spending part of what you should be saving if the whole income came into your account.

Automating your savings and investing will put you on a path to a successful retirement life, and getting out of debt enhances your peace because you'll no longer have to worry about paying your bills on time. It will also help to build your confidence level and help you make good career and business decisions because your choices will no longer be driven by fear caused by the debts you owe. Peaceful living in financial terms means living without debt burden, and having a savings and investment plan that will provide you a future you desire.

Chapter 5

"It's not how much money you make, but how much money you keep, how hard it works for you, and how many generations you keep it for." —*Robert Kiyosaki*

5.1 Save like a pro

I enjoy the game of soccer. I play the game from time to time, whenever I have the opportunity to do so, but I'm particularly ecstatic watching professional soccer players on the pitch playing the game I love. I enjoy seeing them dribble, maneuver, run with the ball, attack or defend, and ultimately score goals. An average spectator may be imagining how these pros play effortlessly. They make it seem easy because they have mastered the game due to the hours of training and coaching they've received. Saving money can be the same if you learn how to do it, and you empower yourself to put it into practice. You'll then be able to get the benefits of saving money and building wealth. By following the practical steps laid out in the next section, you will earn the power to save.

5.2 Practical steps to automating like a pro

Saving money starts with your mindset. You must first understand the need to save, and attach a purpose to your saving. Having a goal for the money you're putting in your savings account will provide you the motivation and drive to fulfill the goals. For example, maybe your old car is in a bad shape, and it can totally pack up at any moment. You know a new car is a must, and by creating a car savings plan, the necessity of a new car will be your drive to stick to your savings plan. This is because if you fail to save, you will not be able to buy the car, and you may invariably put yourself in a position where you have no vehicle to take you around. In the same way, if your plan is to save for a long-term goal like retirement, you're thinking about a future state, and it's only by understanding the importance of having a comfortable retirement life that you will be able to consistently save for that purpose.

Below are five practical steps to make saving easier and automate like a pro.

1. <u>Evaluate your income</u>: If you're expecting to see ways to cut down your expenses, sorry to disappoint. I focused on that aspect in my book *Money Equation*, which you can check out. It's always good to control your expenses to fit your income, but I think it's way better to increase your income, and to match your desired lifestyle by creating multiple sources of passive income. If you want to learn more about how to generate passive income, read Volume 1 of this series which covers how to earn money.

   By evaluating your income, you'll be able to review if what you earn is sufficient to maintain your standard of living. If you found out that this isn't the case, you can either cut your expenses, or find ways to increase your income. For an underearner, it will be difficult to save any money because their income is already too low to cover their living expenses. The solution is to find other ways to make more money. For other people whose income can easily cover their basic needs, saving should also become a little easier. And to save like a pro, you need to take a holistic approach by apportioning your income to cover your expenses — both wants and needs — without sacrificing your savings. You must make saving a priority.

2. <u>Use direct deposit to power up your savings</u>: You need to make the decision about how much you want to save per paycheck even before your salary gets into your account. That is the surefire way of empowering yourself to save. If you've made your decision about the amount or percentage of your income that you want to save, you must also make sure you honor your decision by committing to the routine. Most employers in the US let you enroll in direct deposit deduction from your salary. With this tool, you can save a certain percentage in your employer's sponsored 401(k) contribution for your retirement. This gives you the opportunity to save, and at the same time invest your money for the future. If you don't have any form of retirement savings plan in your organization, you can still take advantage of a direct deposit deduction by giving your employer instruction on which account and what amount of

your salary to deposit. Typically, you can have two or more bank accounts set up to receive your salary. Have one of the accounts dedicated towards savings and investment, while you can use other accounts for your regular expenses.

3. <u>Create saving goals</u>: It is impossible to achieve anything meaningful without having a goal. What are your financial goals? When you save money, make sure you're saving not just because everyone else does, but because you have a specific plan you want to accomplish. After creating the plan, you need to figure out how much money you will need and how long it might take you to save it. You should have short-term savings goals to take care of expenses that you plan to accomplish within a year. This may include replacing a household appliance like a TV or dishwasher. Your medium-term saving goals should take care of expenditures that should happen within two to five years. This may include changing your car or saving for a home down payment. Your long-term saving goals are meant to take care of your child's education, and your retirement. When setting your money goal, you should make sure that your short-term goal is not robbing you of your future plans, and also don't let your future goals deny your of the short-term needs.

4. <u>Build your system</u>: When it comes to money management, I've observed that there is no one-size-fits-all approach to saving. It all depends on the lifestyle you want to lead, and your priorities. While some are happy to spend money on expensive cars and live in a modest home, others prefer to drive cheaper cars and live in expensive neighborhoods because of the access to great school system. It is all about your priorities. However, you must make sure that you prioritize savings, and don't let your lifestyle put you into debt.

Many of the money experts out there have several conflicting recommendations in terms of how to allocate your money. Some are in support of the 50/30/20 rule, which states that you should target to spend 50% of your income on needs, 30% on wants, and save 20%. Others believe the ratio should be 60/20/10. We live in a world where housing and food prices are increasing faster than your income, so how can you really keep up with these percentages? My thought is that you should build a financial management system that works for you, and the system must allow you to prioritize savings by socking away at least 10% of your income in your savings account. You need a mechanism that will allow your money to make more money for you, and that is the purpose of the 10%. If 10% is not easy for you, you should try to boost your income by asking for a raise from your employer, changing jobs, starting a side hustle, getting more customers if you are a business owner, or reducing your living expenses.

5. Reward yourself: Professional athletes get paid a lot, and they get rewarded after winning their tournaments. You can apply this concept to your saving goals as well, whether you are paying off a debt, or paying cash for a new car. You should reward yourself when you set big goals and accomplish them. You can also determine what the reward should be. You may decide to take a long overdue vacation, eat out in an expensive restaurant, go for a massage, or splurge and buy something really nice for yourself. The reward will keep you motivated and help you focus on your next important goal. Rewarding yourself is a way of acknowledging the sacrifice that you have made to achieve your money goal, and it helps make it fun to save money.

5.3 Join the Money Finder Challenge

There are quite a number of people that wrestle with how to save money. They know they need to save money, but they are not sure of how to go about it. They don't know what steps to take and how to organize their finances in order to create a savings plan that is easily implementable.

When I was teaching my first daughter how to ride a bicycle, I took her through a step-by-step guide on how to do it. With her helmet on her head, I made sure she sat comfortably on the bike's saddle. I told her to hold on to the handlebars with her two arms stretched forward, head lifted with eyes looking straight ahead. I then put her two feet on the pedals of the bicycle and told her to start moving her legs in a clockwise motion. As she pedaled, the bicycle started forward. She was excited to see that she could ride a bike! Of course, the training wheel was on, but I could feel the confidence and the sense of accomplishment that my three-year-old daughter experienced riding that day.

Just like my three-year-old daughter, many people need that guidance with saving money. They are adults, but they still need someone to help them figure out how to plan and manage their finances. It's not their fault that they don't know how. It is the lack of financial education in our academic institutions that has caused people to mismanage their money.

For this reason, I created the Money Finder Challenge. In this exciting challenge, I will take you through 10 days of fun activities to help you figure out how to save more money from your current income. To join this challenge, go here: https://www.winnersways.com/find-more-money-in-just-10-days/.

5.4 Strategies and mindset to create a smart saving plan

Most people are not able to save because they associate pain and restrictions to it. They know that saving is a way of delaying gratification, but they want their pleasure right now. They know that being in debt is not good for their financial standing, but they don't know how to avoid it. They want to live a happy life that is free of money worries, but they are not sure of the strategies that will help them get to their financial nirvana. The case of Mr. Cloudy and Mr. Bloomy is a classic example of what differentiates people with a wealthy mindset from the poor ones.

Mr. Cloudy, a medical doctor, earns $300,000 each year, which makes him among the top 1% earners in America, but he still finds it difficult to balance his budget. He still complains that he is not earning enough money and he often relies on credit cards to make ends meet. Mr. Cloudy lives in an affluent neighborhood with a gate and he still has over $420,000 left on his mortgage. His two children go to private schools, which cost him around $60,000 every year. He has nothing saved for their college education, but he plans to help pay for their college tuition. He is obsessed with cars, and he changes his every two to three years. According to him, "The smell of a new car makes me feel satisfied and happy." He has a boat and a truck that he uses occasionally, but pays bills on them every month just to display them in his yard. Mr. Cloudy is in his early forties. He is not thinking of retirement at the moment because he thinks he still has many more years to catch up and save, and he has just around $50,000 in his retirement accounts. Mr. Cloudy is definitely an intelligent and hardworking man, and he makes a lot of money, but he lacks the financial sense of saving or budgeting.

Mr. Bloomy, who is an engineer, earns $200,000 each year. He is a better money manager than Mr. Cloudy because he regularly uses his budget to guide his monthly expenses. He has been a dedicated budgeter for over a decade. He saves money regularly by always paying himself first, and any item that cannot be covered in his budget in any particular month he postpones or discards. He also lives in a gated community, but he has less than $200,000 left on his home mortgage and he is on track to pay off his home loans in about seven years. His three children attend the local public schools, and he is funding their college savings account so that they will have enough money by the time they are ready for college. Mr. Bloomy and his wife both drive used cars, they have no car loans, and no debt in any way, shape, or form, other than their outstanding mortgage loan. He is a thirty-eight-year-old man with over $450,000 saved in his retirement account, and he is financially savvy because he is deliberate with all his expenses. The Bloomy family has peace because they know how to manage their money.

The difference between these two families is in their mindset. The two families are both hardworking American families. One family is on track to achieve the true American dream of owning a home and retiring in dignity, while the other family is caught up in the rat race of trying to keep up with the Joneses. The have different mindsets about how to handle their income. One family spends everything they make to impress people without saving enough money for a rainy day, while the other family carefully plans their spending, letting their budget guide their priorities.

What kind of mindset do you need to win in the game of money? Can anyone become wealthy? Are there principles or qualities that I need to be aware of in order to become wealthy? These and more are the questions that I asked myself as I began my journey to a life of financial freedom. I read lots of books, listened to teachings, and spoke with many people that are already free financially. The central message from my research is that anyone can fundamentally become wealthy, but they need to work on their mindset and belief system.

Below are seven core mindsets that are associated with financially free people:

1. <u>They have a wealth mindset</u>: The starting point for every achievement is from our mind, and before you can achieve anything, you have to first belief that you have the capacity to attain such. People that are financially free have been able to defeat limiting beliefs that are associated with poor and middle-class people. Some of the limiting beliefs that you need to eradicate in order to become wealthy include believing that:

   - Money is the root of all evil.
   - Wealthy people are not honest people.
   - I am not smart enough to make a lot of money.
   - It is selfish to want a lot of money.
   - You have to work too hard to make a lot of money.
   - You have to sacrifice many good things in order to make money.
   - Wealthy people are not happy people.

2. <u>They make financial abundance a must</u>: When most people think or talk about money, they assess money or wealth from the standpoint of survival. They only consider what they need to do in order to feed themselves, pay their bills, and maintain the minimum living condition. Financially free people operate on a different perspective. They think and aim for financial abundance. They work towards having more than what can take care of their immediate needs.

They also have a long-term view of the kind of life they want, and they develop plans that will make them become financially secure. Do you want to become financially free? Then you need to make financial abundance a must. Stop thinking or living in survival mode.

3. They have role models: In the opening chapters, I wrote about how our school systems have failed in providing our children the proper financial education that will help them manage their money. Most parents are also unable to pass the right knowledge onto their children because they are also struggling to make ends meet, and they do not have role models in their lives to help them. In my research, I found out that the majority of millionaires around us are self-made millionaires, and having a role model played a huge role in helping them become financially free. The technological era of today has made it far easier to connect with people you would otherwise not be able to reach. If you want to learn how to manage your money, find role models from whom you can learn best practices. For example, if you want to be an entrepreneur, connect with people like Daymond John, Mark Cuban, Elon Musk, or any entrepreneur that you admire and respect. If you want to achieve your financial freedom as an investor, then you should connect with investing gurus like Bill Ackman, Charlie Munger, Warren Buffett, or any other investor that you can consider a role model. Follow them, learn from them, listen to their interviews, and you will be able to pick their brain and start your own journey.

4. They have a strategy: Nothing happens by accident. Financially rich people obtain their status through deliberate and strategic planning. After choosing your role model, you need to come up with your own set of strategies that will help you achieve your financial goals. You learned from your role models about wining strategies and you have some knowledge about what works for them. For example, I follow Warren Buffett, and I know he is a value

investor. He looks for good stock at a bargain price in companies that have strong competitive advantages and solid management teams. He invests in companies that he is ready to hold for the long term. If you adopt best practices as you develop your strategies, you will achieve optimum results.

There is a huge difference between having information and acting on the information. Many people theoretically know what they need to do in order to achieve financial freedom. They know they must earn an income, they know that they ought to save and invest, they know that they are supposed to live within their means, and they know they should have a budget to plan their monthly spending. But they are not achieving results because they only *know* — they did not *act*. You must follow through with your strategies so that you can have your desired outcome.

5. <u>They know that money is a slave</u>: The way the rich view money is totally different from the way poor people and the middle-class see money. Poor people work very hard to make money, while the affluent make money work hard for them. I learned this principle not too long ago, and I have started practicing it and making my money my slave. From every paycheck that I receive, I have automated my savings such that a certain amount goes into my savings account. From there, it goes into some form of investment so that it can now work for me and produce more money.

That is the secret sauce: You need to know how to make your money work for you, whether you are awake or asleep. If you know how to properly deploy your money into the right investment vehicle, it will continue to work tirelessly for you, making you richer. Now I set goals on how much passive income I want to make every year using my money to generate more money for me. To become financially free, you must find a way to make your money work for you. The harder you can let it work for you, the quicker you will get to your goals. Stop chasing money all around. Change your mindset today, and start making your money work for you.

6. They get rich slowly: Our society has been hoodwinked into the fallacy that there is such a thing as overnight success. We have been made to believe in the "get rich quick" approach: you just need to invest or show up somewhere, and you will start generating enough returns to make you wealthy. I hate to burst your bubble, but the number of early or young millionaires are minuscule when compared with people that got there slowly. An overwhelming majority of the people I researched explained that it takes on average about two decades from when they started making intentional decisions about money before they became financially free. What we see on television or read on social media are just cases of outliers that is not applicable to the majority. So when you start the journey towards financial freedom, I want you to know that it will take some time. You will have to stay consistent even when you are not seeing immediate results, because there is no such thing as overnight wealth. If you doubt this statement, go and ask an average lottery winner. Many of them have gone from nothing to suddenly becoming an overnight millionaire, and many of them have lost the same money the same way — suddenly.

7. They give more than they take: This may sound counterintuitive, but from my study, I also realized that giving is one of the mindsets of wealthy people. They thrive in giving, they work to make life easier for other people, and they readily serve others without any expectation of getting anything in return. I am still amazed at the amounts billionaires and millionaires like Michael Bloomberg, Bill Gates, Warren Buffett, and many others have pledged to give during their lifetime — out of their own money. You may not have all the money in the world, but a winning mindset is also a giving mindset. You should find someone

that you can be a blessing to by giving them something that will be of value to them. It does not necessarily have to be in financial terms. You can give your time, your service, or you can give by just taking time to listen to other people, especially when they go through difficult times.

"Money is only a tool. It will take you wherever you wish, but it will not replace you as the driver." —*Ayn Rand*

Take-Away: Empowered to Save

This concludes Book 2 of the *Your Money. Your Slave.* series. You have learned that you must make paying yourself a priority to be an effective money manager. The money that you pay yourself is what you will eventually use to build your wealth, and you do this by making your money work harder than you worked to earn it. You know that you have to become intentional and take control of your money in order to possess the power to save. And that budgeting your money is a way of empowering yourself to acquire that control.

I explained that debt robs you of your future potential opportunities and I shared tips that will make you financially fit. We also explored the differences between being cheap and being frugal. It's good to be frugal, but don't be cheap. Cheap people are often times a penny wise, but a pound foolish. That means that they waste more money in the long run, when they actually think they are saving money. By automating your money, you now realize that you can save like a pro.

The purpose of this eBook *Power to Save* is to help put you on a path to financial prosperity. We all work very hard to make money and to prosper financially, and we must be able to make our money work harder to earn more money for us. The starting point in making money work for us is to systematically deploy our money into profitable ventures that will continue to make money for us whether we are asleep or wide awake.

This book has shared ideas and strategies to guide you in taking that first step to save money. You however have to be intentional and purposeful about your savings. You must make sure that you are not just packing money in your bank account because you want to have a number with multiple zeros behind it. You must save with a goal and a purpose.

Power to Save is meant to be your go-to guide when you want to learn about the mentality and strategies for saving money. Saving is not about denying yourself the good things of life, but empowering yourself to prioritize your wants and create a savings plan to help you fulfill your desires. The Bible says that the rich rule over the poor, and the borrower is a slave to the lender. To prosper financially, you must avoid putting yourself in debt. This book is your guide to breaking the shackle of debt, poverty, and lack mentality. It will put you on a path to financial prosperity. Thank you for reading.

Congratulations! You are now empowered to save. Watch out for Book 3 of the Money Power series, to learn how to invest your money to create more money for you.

I write about Personal Finance: Sign up for my newsletter at www.winnersways.com

Power to Save: Putting you on a path to financial prosperity.